Who Came to My Party? and What Did They Bring?

©2018 Cris Rariden

PARTY!   PARTY! PARTY!

Birthday Parties	Retirement Parties
Baby Showers	Bridal Showers
Easter	Thanksgiving
Christmas	New Year's Eve
Fourth of July	Mother's Day
Father's Day	Memorial Day
Labor Day	First Communions
First Day of School	Last Day of School
Graduations	Random Gatherings
Game Night	Card Parties
Halloween Parties	Bon Voyage Parties

Parties! If we are lucky, our lives are filled with parties. People with large families and a lot of friends might attend dozens of parties every year. As time goes by, instead of trying to guess who brought what and who showed up, it's nice to have a **Party Journal for The Record**.

Three or four years down the road you may not remember what you gave or received as a gift. A few years from now, you might wonder who's turn it is to host Thanksgiving or Easter or Christmas.

This is where the **Party Journal** will come in handy. It can also be a nice reminiscing tool at a future party that might be heading south. It's a reminder of the Fun Times! The Party Times!

Most of your information will fit on a single page, but for a BIG party, go ahead and use two or more pages until everyone is accounted for!

This Journal is dedicated to the Record Keeper in the family.

The Occasion: _____

Date: _____ Where: _____Time: _____

What was served: _____

Who Attended and What Did They Bring?   Food and/ or Gifts

On a scale of 1- 10, how successful was the gathering: _____

Games played: _____

Disagreements or arguments: _____

Other Notes: _____

_____

_____

_____

The Occasion: _____

Date: _____ Where: _____Time: _____

What was served: _____

Who Attended and What Did They Bring?   Food and/ or Gifts

On a scale of 1- 10, how successful was the gathering: _____

Games played: _____

Disagreements or arguments: _____

Other Notes: _____

_____

_____

_____

The Occasion: _____

Date: _____ Where: _____Time: _____

What was served: _____

Who Attended and What Did They Bring?   Food and/ or Gifts

On a scale of 1- 10, how successful was the gathering: _____

Games played: _____

Disagreements or arguments: _____

Other Notes: _____

_____

_____

_____

The Occasion: _____

Date: _____ Where: _____Time: _____

What was served: _____

Who Attended and What Did They Bring?   Food and/ or Gifts

On a scale of 1- 10, how successful was the gathering: _____

Games played: _____

Disagreements or arguments: _____

Other Notes: _____

_____

_____

_____

The Occasion: _____

Date: _____ Where: _____Time: _____

What was served: _____

Who Attended and What Did They Bring?   Food and/ or Gifts

On a scale of 1- 10, how successful was the gathering: _____

Games played: _____

Disagreements or arguments: _____

Other Notes: _____

_____

_____

_____

The Occasion: _____

Date: _____ Where: _____ Time: _____

What was served: _____

Who Attended and What Did They Bring?   Food and/ or Gifts

On a scale of 1- 10, how successful was the gathering: _____

Games played: _____

Disagreements or arguments: _____

Other Notes: _____

_____

_____

_____

The Occasion: _____

Date: _____ Where: _____Time: _____

What was served: _____

Who Attended and What Did They Bring?   Food and/ or Gifts

On a scale of 1- 10, how successful was the gathering: _____

Games played: _____

Disagreements or arguments: _____

Other Notes: _____

_____

_____

_____

The Occasion: _____

Date: _____ Where: _____Time: _____

What was served: _____

Who Attended and What Did They Bring?   Food and/ or Gifts

On a scale of 1- 10, how successful was the gathering: _____

Games played: _____

Disagreements or arguments: _____

Other Notes: _____

_____

_____

_____

The Occasion: _____

Date: _____ Where: _____Time: _____

What was served: _____

Who Attended and What Did They Bring?   Food and/ or Gifts

On a scale of 1- 10, how successful was the gathering: _____

Games played: _____

Disagreements or arguments: _____

Other Notes: _____

_____

_____

_____

The Occasion: _____

Date: _____ Where: _____Time: _____

What was served: _____

Who Attended and What Did They Bring?   Food and/ or Gifts

On a scale of 1- 10, how successful was the gathering: _____

Games played: _____

Disagreements or arguments: _____

Other Notes: _____

_____

_____

_____

The Occasion: _____

Date: _____ Where: _____Time: _____

What was served: _____

Who Attended and What Did They Bring?   Food and/ or Gifts

On a scale of 1- 10, how successful was the gathering: _____

Games played: _____

Disagreements or arguments: _____

Other Notes: _____

_____

_____

_____

The Occasion: _____

Date: _____ Where: _____Time: _____

What was served: _____

Who Attended and What Did They Bring?   Food and/ or Gifts

On a scale of 1- 10, how successful was the gathering: _____

Games played: _____

Disagreements or arguments: _____

Other Notes: _____

_____

_____

_____

The Occasion: _____

Date: _____ Where: _____Time: _____

What was served: _____

Who Attended and What Did They Bring?   Food and/ or Gifts

On a scale of 1- 10, how successful was the gathering: _____

Games played: _____

Disagreements or arguments: _____

Other Notes: _____

_____

_____

_____

The Occasion: _____

Date: _____ Where: _____Time: _____

What was served: _____

Who Attended and What Did They Bring?   Food and/ or Gifts

On a scale of 1- 10, how successful was the gathering: _____

Games played: _____

Disagreements or arguments: _____

Other Notes: _____

_____

_____

_____

The Occasion: _____

Date: _____ Where: _____Time: _____

What was served: _____

Who Attended and What Did They Bring?   Food and/ or Gifts

On a scale of 1- 10, how successful was the gathering: _____

Games played: _____

Disagreements or arguments: _____

Other Notes: _____

_____

_____

_____

The Occasion: _____

Date: _____ Where: _____Time: _____

What was served: _____

Who Attended and What Did They Bring?   Food and/ or Gifts

On a scale of 1- 10, how successful was the gathering: _____

Games played: _____

Disagreements or arguments: _____

Other Notes: _____

_____

_____

_____

The Occasion: _____

Date: _____ Where: _____Time: _____

What was served: _____

Who Attended and What Did They Bring?   Food and/ or Gifts

On a scale of 1- 10, how successful was the gathering: _____

Games played: _____

Disagreements or arguments: _____

Other Notes: _____

_____

_____

_____

The Occasion: _____

Date: _____ Where: _____Time: _____

What was served: _____

Who Attended and What Did They Bring?   Food and/ or Gifts

On a scale of 1- 10, how successful was the gathering: _____

Games played: _____

Disagreements or arguments: _____

Other Notes: _____

_____

_____

_____

The Occasion: _____

Date: _____ Where: _____Time: _____

What was served: _____

Who Attended and What Did They Bring?   Food and/ or Gifts

On a scale of 1- 10, how successful was the gathering: _____

Games played: _____

Disagreements or arguments: _____

Other Notes: _____

_____

_____

_____

The Occasion: _____

Date: _____ Where: _____Time: _____

What was served: _____

Who Attended and What Did They Bring?   Food and/ or Gifts

On a scale of 1- 10, how successful was the gathering: _____

Games played: _____

Disagreements or arguments: _____

Other Notes: _____

_____

_____

_____

The Occasion: _____

Date: _____ Where: _____Time: _____

What was served: _____

Who Attended and What Did They Bring?   Food and/ or Gifts

On a scale of 1- 10, how successful was the gathering: _____

Games played: _____

Disagreements or arguments: _____

Other Notes: _____

_____

_____

_____

The Occasion: _____

Date: _____ Where: _____Time: _____

What was served: _____

Who Attended and What Did They Bring?   Food and/ or Gifts

On a scale of 1- 10, how successful was the gathering: _____

Games played: _____

Disagreements or arguments: _____

Other Notes: _____

_____

_____

_____

The Occasion: _____

Date: _____ Where: _____Time: _____

What was served: _____

Who Attended and What Did They Bring?   Food and/ or Gifts

On a scale of 1- 10, how successful was the gathering: _____

Games played: _____

Disagreements or arguments: _____

Other Notes: _____

_____

_____

_____

The Occasion: _____

Date: _____ Where: _____Time: _____

What was served: _____

Who Attended and What Did They Bring?   Food and/ or Gifts

On a scale of 1- 10, how successful was the gathering: _____

Games played: _____

Disagreements or arguments: _____

Other Notes: _____

_____

_____

_____

The Occasion: _____

Date: _____ Where: _____Time: _____

What was served: _____

Who Attended and What Did They Bring?   Food and/ or Gifts

On a scale of 1- 10, how successful was the gathering: _____

Games played: _____

Disagreements or arguments: _____

Other Notes: _____

_____

_____

_____

The Occasion: _____

Date: _____ Where: _____Time: _____

What was served: _____

Who Attended and What Did They Bring?   Food and/ or Gifts

On a scale of 1- 10, how successful was the gathering: _____

Games played: _____

Disagreements or arguments: _____

Other Notes: _____

_____

_____

_____

The Occasion: _____

Date: _____ Where: _____ Time: _____

What was served: _____

Who Attended and What Did They Bring?   Food and/ or Gifts

On a scale of 1- 10, how successful was the gathering: _____

Games played: _____

Disagreements or arguments: _____

Other Notes: _____

_____

_____

_____

The Occasion: _____

Date: _____ Where: _____ Time: _____

What was served: _____

Who Attended and What Did They Bring?   Food and/ or Gifts

On a scale of 1- 10, how successful was the gathering: _____

Games played: _____

Disagreements or arguments: _____

Other Notes: _____

_____

_____

_____

The Occasion: _____

Date: _____ Where: _____Time: _____

What was served: _____

Who Attended and What Did They Bring?   Food and/ or Gifts

On a scale of 1- 10, how successful was the gathering: _____

Games played: _____

Disagreements or arguments: _____

Other Notes: _____

_____

_____

_____

The Occasion: _____

Date: _____ Where: _____Time: _____

What was served: _____

Who Attended and What Did They Bring?   Food and/ or Gifts

On a scale of 1- 10, how successful was the gathering: _____

Games played: _____

Disagreements or arguments: _____

Other Notes: _____

_____

_____

_____

The Occasion: _____

Date: _____ Where: _____Time: _____

What was served: _____

Who Attended and What Did They Bring?   Food and/ or Gifts

On a scale of 1- 10, how successful was the gathering: _____

Games played: _____

Disagreements or arguments: _____

Other Notes: _____

_____

_____

_____

The Occasion: _____

Date: _____ Where: _____ Time: _____

What was served: _____

Who Attended and What Did They Bring?   Food and/ or Gifts

On a scale of 1- 10, how successful was the gathering: _____

Games played: _____

Disagreements or arguments: _____

Other Notes: _____

_____

_____

_____

The Occasion: _____

Date: _____ Where: _____Time: _____

What was served: _____

Who Attended and What Did They Bring?   Food and/ or Gifts

On a scale of 1- 10, how successful was the gathering: _____

Games played: _____

Disagreements or arguments: _____

Other Notes: _____

_____

_____

_____

The Occasion: _____

Date: _____ Where: _____Time: _____

What was served: _____

Who Attended and What Did They Bring?   Food and/ or Gifts

On a scale of 1- 10, how successful was the gathering: _____

Games played: _____

Disagreements or arguments: _____

Other Notes: _____

_____

_____

_____

The Occasion: _____

Date: _____ Where: _____Time: _____

What was served: _____

Who Attended and What Did They Bring?   Food and/ or Gifts

On a scale of 1- 10, how successful was the gathering: _____

Games played: _____

Disagreements or arguments: _____

Other Notes: _____

_____

_____

_____

The Occasion: _____

Date: _____ Where: _____Time: _____

What was served: _____

Who Attended and What Did They Bring?   Food and/ or Gifts

On a scale of 1- 10, how successful was the gathering: _____

Games played: _____

Disagreements or arguments: _____

Other Notes: _____

_____

_____

_____

The Occasion: _____

Date: _____ Where: _____Time: _____

What was served: _____

Who Attended and What Did They Bring?   Food and/ or Gifts

On a scale of 1- 10, how successful was the gathering: _____

Games played: _____

Disagreements or arguments: _____

Other Notes: _____

_____

_____

_____

The Occasion: _____

Date: _____ Where: _____Time: _____

What was served: _____

Who Attended and What Did They Bring?   Food and/ or Gifts

On a scale of 1- 10, how successful was the gathering: _____

Games played: _____

Disagreements or arguments: _____

Other Notes: _____

_____

_____

_____

The Occasion: _____

Date: _____ Where: _____Time: _____

What was served: _____

Who Attended and What Did They Bring?   Food and/ or Gifts

On a scale of 1-10, how successful was the gathering: _____

Games played: _____

Disagreements or arguments: _____

Other Notes: _____

_____

_____

_____

The Occasion: _____

Date: _____ Where: _____Time: _____

What was served: _____

Who Attended and What Did They Bring?   Food and/ or Gifts

On a scale of 1- 10, how successful was the gathering: _____

Games played: _____

Disagreements or arguments: _____

Other Notes: _____

_____

_____

_____

The Occasion: _____

Date: _____ Where: _____Time: _____

What was served: _____

Who Attended and What Did They Bring?   Food and/ or Gifts

On a scale of 1- 10, how successful was the gathering: _____

Games played: _____

Disagreements or arguments: _____

Other Notes: _____

_____

_____

_____

The Occasion: _____

Date: _____ Where: _____Time: _____

What was served: _____

Who Attended and What Did They Bring?   Food and/ or Gifts

On a scale of 1- 10, how successful was the gathering: _____

Games played: _____

Disagreements or arguments: _____

Other Notes: _____

_____

_____

_____

The Occasion: _____

Date: _____ Where: _____Time: _____

What was served: _____

Who Attended and What Did They Bring?   Food and/ or Gifts

On a scale of 1- 10, how successful was the gathering: _____

Games played: _____

Disagreements or arguments: _____

Other Notes: _____

_____

_____

_____

The Occasion: _____

Date: _____ Where: _____Time: _____

What was served: _____

Who Attended and What Did They Bring?   Food and/ or Gifts

On a scale of 1- 10, how successful was the gathering: _____

Games played: _____

Disagreements or arguments: _____

Other Notes: _____

_____

_____

_____

The Occasion: _____

Date: _____ Where: _____Time: _____

What was served: _____

Who Attended and What Did They Bring?   Food and/ or Gifts

On a scale of 1-10, how successful was the gathering: _____

Games played: _____

Disagreements or arguments: _____

Other Notes: _____

_____

_____

_____

The Occasion: _____

Date: _____ Where: _____Time: _____

What was served: _____

Who Attended and What Did They Bring?   Food and/ or Gifts

On a scale of 1- 10, how successful was the gathering: _____

Games played: _____

Disagreements or arguments: _____

Other Notes: _____

_____

_____

_____

The Occasion: _____

Date: _____ Where: _____ Time: _____

What was served: _____

Who Attended and What Did They Bring?   Food and/ or Gifts

On a scale of 1- 10, how successful was the gathering: _____

Games played: _____

Disagreements or arguments: _____

Other Notes: _____

_____

_____

_____

The Occasion: _____

Date: _____ Where: _____ Time: _____

What was served: _____

Who Attended and What Did They Bring?   Food and/ or Gifts

On a scale of 1- 10, how successful was the gathering: _____

Games played: _____

Disagreements or arguments: _____

Other Notes: _____

_____

_____

_____

The Occasion: _____

Date: _____ Where: _____Time: _____

What was served: _____

Who Attended and What Did They Bring?   Food and/ or Gifts

On a scale of 1- 10, how successful was the gathering: _____

Games played: _____

Disagreements or arguments: _____

Other Notes: _____

_____

_____

_____

The Occasion: _____

Date: _____ Where: _____Time: _____

What was served: _____

Who Attended and What Did They Bring?   Food and/ or Gifts

On a scale of 1- 10, how successful was the gathering: _____

Games played: _____

Disagreements or arguments: _____

Other Notes: _____

_____

_____

_____

The Occasion: _____

Date: _____ Where: _____Time: _____

What was served: _____

Who Attended and What Did They Bring?   Food and/ or Gifts

On a scale of 1- 10, how successful was the gathering: _____

Games played: _____

Disagreements or arguments: _____

Other Notes: _____

_____

_____

_____

The Occasion: _____

Date: _____ Where: _____Time: _____

What was served: _____

Who Attended and What Did They Bring?   Food and/ or Gifts

On a scale of 1- 10, how successful was the gathering: _____

Games played: _____

Disagreements or arguments: _____

Other Notes: _____

_____

_____

_____

The Occasion: _____

Date: _____ Where: _____Time: _____

What was served: _____

Who Attended and What Did They Bring?   Food and/ or Gifts

On a scale of 1- 10, how successful was the gathering: _____

Games played: _____

Disagreements or arguments: _____

Other Notes: _____

_____

_____

_____

The Occasion: _____

Date: _____ Where: _____Time: _____

What was served: _____

Who Attended and What Did They Bring?   Food and/ or Gifts

On a scale of 1- 10, how successful was the gathering: _____

Games played: _____

Disagreements or arguments: _____

Other Notes: _____

_____

_____

_____

The Occasion: _____

Date: _____ Where: _____Time: _____

What was served: _____

Who Attended and What Did They Bring?   Food and/ or Gifts

On a scale of 1- 10, how successful was the gathering: _____

Games played: _____

Disagreements or arguments: _____

Other Notes: _____

_____

_____

_____

The Occasion: _____

Date: _____ Where: _____Time: _____

What was served: _____

Who Attended and What Did They Bring?   Food and/ or Gifts

On a scale of 1- 10, how successful was the gathering: _____

Games played: _____

Disagreements or arguments: _____

Other Notes: _____

_____

_____

_____

The Occasion: _____

Date: _____ Where: _____Time: _____

What was served: _____

Who Attended and What Did They Bring?   Food and/ or Gifts

On a scale of 1- 10, how successful was the gathering: _____

Games played: _____

Disagreements or arguments: _____

Other Notes: _____

_____

_____

_____

The Occasion: _____

Date: _____ Where: _____Time: _____

What was served: _____

Who Attended and What Did They Bring?   Food and/ or Gifts

On a scale of 1- 10, how successful was the gathering: _____

Games played: _____

Disagreements or arguments: _____

Other Notes: _____

_____

_____

_____

The Occasion: _____

Date: _____ Where: _____Time: _____

What was served: _____

Who Attended and What Did They Bring?   Food and/ or Gifts

On a scale of 1- 10, how successful was the gathering: _____

Games played: _____

Disagreements or arguments: _____

Other Notes: _____

_____

_____

_____

The Occasion: _____

Date: _____ Where: _____Time: _____

What was served: _____

Who Attended and What Did They Bring?   Food and/ or Gifts

On a scale of 1- 10, how successful was the gathering: _____

Games played: _____

Disagreements or arguments: _____

Other Notes: _____

_____

_____

_____

The Occasion: _____

Date: _____ Where: _____Time: _____

What was served: _____

Who Attended and What Did They Bring?   Food and/ or Gifts

On a scale of 1- 10, how successful was the gathering: _____

Games played: _____

Disagreements or arguments: _____

Other Notes: _____

_____

_____

_____

The Occasion: _____

Date: _____ Where: _____Time: _____

What was served: _____

Who Attended and What Did They Bring?   Food and/ or Gifts

On a scale of 1- 10, how successful was the gathering: _____

Games played: _____

Disagreements or arguments: _____

Other Notes: _____

_____

_____

_____

The Occasion: _____

Date: _____ Where: _____Time: _____

What was served: _____

Who Attended and What Did They Bring?   Food and/ or Gifts

On a scale of 1- 10, how successful was the gathering: _____

Games played: _____

Disagreements or arguments: _____

Other Notes: _____

_____

_____

_____

The Occasion: _____

Date: _____ Where: _____Time: _____

What was served: _____

Who Attended and What Did They Bring?   Food and/ or Gifts

On a scale of 1- 10, how successful was the gathering: _____

Games played: _____

Disagreements or arguments: _____

Other Notes: _____

_____

_____

_____

The Occasion: _____

Date: _____ Where: _____ Time: _____

What was served: _____

Who Attended and What Did They Bring?   Food and/ or Gifts

On a scale of 1- 10, how successful was the gathering: _____

Games played: _____

Disagreements or arguments: _____

Other Notes: _____

_____

_____

_____

The Occasion: _____

Date: _____ Where: _____Time: _____

What was served: _____

Who Attended and What Did They Bring?   Food and/ or Gifts

On a scale of 1- 10, how successful was the gathering: _____

Games played: _____

Disagreements or arguments: _____

Other Notes: _____

_____

_____

_____

The Occasion: _____

Date: _____ Where: _____Time: _____

What was served: _____

Who Attended and What Did They Bring?   Food and/ or Gifts

On a scale of 1- 10, how successful was the gathering: _____

Games played: _____

Disagreements or arguments: _____

Other Notes: _____

_____

_____

_____

The Occasion: _____

Date: _____ Where: _____ Time: _____

What was served: _____

Who Attended and What Did They Bring?   Food and/ or Gifts

On a scale of 1- 10, how successful was the gathering: _____

Games played: _____

Disagreements or arguments: _____

Other Notes: _____

_____

_____

_____

The Occasion: _____

Date: _____ Where: _____Time: _____

What was served: _____

Who Attended and What Did They Bring?   Food and/ or Gifts

Who Attended and What Did They Bring?	Food and/ or Gifts

On a scale of 1- 10, how successful was the gathering: _____

Games played: _____

Disagreements or arguments: _____

Other Notes: _____

_____

_____

_____

The Occasion: _____

Date: _____ Where: _____Time: _____

What was served: _____

Who Attended and What Did They Bring?   Food and/ or Gifts

On a scale of 1- 10, how successful was the gathering: _____

Games played: _____

Disagreements or arguments: _____

Other Notes: _____

_____

_____

_____

The Occasion: _____

Date: _____ Where: _____Time: _____

What was served: _____

Who Attended and What Did They Bring?   Food and/ or Gifts

On a scale of 1- 10, how successful was the gathering: _____

Games played: _____

Disagreements or arguments: _____

Other Notes: _____

_____

_____

_____

The Occasion: _____

Date: _____ Where: _____Time: _____

What was served: _____

Who Attended and What Did They Bring?   Food and/ or Gifts

On a scale of 1- 10, how successful was the gathering: _____

Games played: _____

Disagreements or arguments: _____

Other Notes: _____

_____

_____

_____

The Occasion: _____

Date: _____ Where: _____ Time: _____

What was served: _____

Who Attended and What Did They Bring?   Food and/ or Gifts

On a scale of 1- 10, how successful was the gathering: _____

Games played: _____

Disagreements or arguments: _____

Other Notes: _____

_____

_____

_____

The Occasion: _____

Date: _____ Where: _____Time: _____

What was served: _____

Who Attended and What Did They Bring?   Food and/ or Gifts

On a scale of 1- 10, how successful was the gathering: _____

Games played: _____

Disagreements or arguments: _____

Other Notes: _____

_____

_____

_____

The Occasion: _____

Date: _____ Where: _____Time: _____

What was served: _____

Who Attended and What Did They Bring?   Food and/ or Gifts

On a scale of 1- 10, how successful was the gathering: _____

Games played: _____

Disagreements or arguments: _____

Other Notes: _____

_____

_____

_____

The Occasion: _____

Date: _____ Where: _____Time: _____

What was served: _____

Who Attended and What Did They Bring?   Food and/ or Gifts

On a scale of 1- 10, how successful was the gathering: _____

Games played: _____

Disagreements or arguments: _____

Other Notes: _____

_____

_____

_____

The Occasion: _____

Date: _____ Where: _____Time: _____

What was served: _____

Who Attended and What Did They Bring?   Food and/ or Gifts

On a scale of 1- 10, how successful was the gathering: _____

Games played: _____

Disagreements or arguments: _____

Other Notes: _____

_____

_____

_____

The Occasion: _____

Date: _____ Where: _____Time: _____

What was served: _____

Who Attended and What Did They Bring?   Food and/ or Gifts

On a scale of 1- 10, how successful was the gathering: _____

Games played: _____

Disagreements or arguments: _____

Other Notes: _____

_____

_____

_____

The Occasion: _____

Date: _____ Where: _____Time: _____

What was served: _____

Who Attended and What Did They Bring?   Food and/ or Gifts

On a scale of 1- 10, how successful was the gathering: _____

Games played: _____

Disagreements or arguments: _____

Other Notes: _____

_____

_____

_____

The Occasion: _____

Date: _____ Where: _____ Time: _____

What was served: _____

Who Attended and What Did They Bring?   Food and/ or Gifts

On a scale of 1- 10, how successful was the gathering: _____

Games played: _____

Disagreements or arguments: _____

Other Notes: _____

_____

_____

_____

The Occasion: _____

Date: _____ Where: _____Time: _____

What was served: _____

Who Attended and What Did They Bring?   Food and/ or Gifts

On a scale of 1- 10, how successful was the gathering: _____

Games played: _____

Disagreements or arguments: _____

Other Notes: _____

_____

_____

_____

The Occasion: _____

Date: _____ Where: _____ Time: _____

What was served: _____

Who Attended and What Did They Bring?   Food and/ or Gifts

On a scale of 1- 10, how successful was the gathering: _____

Games played: _____

Disagreements or arguments: _____

Other Notes: _____

_____

_____

_____

The Occasion: _____

Date: _____ Where: _____Time: _____

What was served: _____

Who Attended and What Did They Bring?   Food and/ or Gifts

On a scale of 1- 10, how successful was the gathering: _____

Games played: _____

Disagreements or arguments: _____

Other Notes: _____

_____

_____

_____

The Occasion: _____

Date: _____ Where: _____Time: _____

What was served: _____

Who Attended and What Did They Bring?   Food and/ or Gifts

On a scale of 1- 10, how successful was the gathering: _____

Games played: _____

Disagreements or arguments: _____

Other Notes: _____

_____

_____

_____

The Occasion: _____

Date: _____ Where: _____Time: _____

What was served: _____

Who Attended and What Did They Bring?   Food and/ or Gifts

Who Attended and What Did They Bring?	Food and/ or Gifts

On a scale of 1- 10, how successful was the gathering: _____

Games played: _____

Disagreements or arguments: _____

Other Notes: _____

_____

_____

_____

The Occasion: _____

Date: _____ Where: _____Time: _____

What was served: _____

Who Attended and What Did They Bring?   Food and/ or Gifts

On a scale of 1- 10, how successful was the gathering: _____

Games played: _____

Disagreements or arguments: _____

Other Notes: _____

_____

_____

_____

The Occasion: _____

Date: _____ Where: _____Time: _____

What was served: _____

Who Attended and What Did They Bring?   Food and/ or Gifts

Who Attended and What Did They Bring?	Food and/ or Gifts

On a scale of 1- 10, how successful was the gathering: _____

Games played: _____

Disagreements or arguments: _____

Other Notes: _____

_____

_____

_____

The Occasion: _____

Date: _____ Where: _____Time: _____

What was served: _____

Who Attended and What Did They Bring?   Food and/ or Gifts

On a scale of 1- 10, how successful was the gathering: _____

Games played: _____

Disagreements or arguments: _____

Other Notes: _____

_____

_____

_____

The Occasion: _____

Date: _____ Where: _____ Time: _____

What was served: _____

Who Attended and What Did They Bring?   Food and/ or Gifts

On a scale of 1- 10, how successful was the gathering: _____

Games played: _____

Disagreements or arguments: _____

Other Notes: _____

_____

_____

_____

The Occasion: _____

Date: _____ Where: _____Time: _____

What was served: _____

Who Attended and What Did They Bring?   Food and/ or Gifts

On a scale of 1- 10, how successful was the gathering: _____

Games played: _____

Disagreements or arguments: _____

Other Notes: _____

_____

_____

_____

The Occasion: _____

Date: _____ Where: _____Time: _____

What was served: _____

Who Attended and What Did They Bring?   Food and/ or Gifts

On a scale of 1- 10, how successful was the gathering: _____

Games played: _____

Disagreements or arguments: _____

Other Notes: _____

_____

_____

_____

The Occasion: _____

Date: _____ Where: _____Time: _____

What was served: _____

Who Attended and What Did They Bring?   Food and/ or Gifts

On a scale of 1- 10, how successful was the gathering: _____

Games played: _____

Disagreements or arguments: _____

Other Notes: _____

_____

_____

_____

The Occasion: _____

Date: _____ Where: _____Time: _____

What was served: _____

Who Attended and What Did They Bring?   Food and/ or Gifts

On a scale of 1- 10, how successful was the gathering: _____

Games played: _____

Disagreements or arguments: _____

Other Notes: _____

_____

_____

_____

The Occasion: _____

Date: _____ Where: _____ Time: _____

What was served: _____

Who Attended and What Did They Bring?   Food and/ or Gifts

On a scale of 1- 10, how successful was the gathering: _____

Games played: _____

Disagreements or arguments: _____

Other Notes: _____

_____

_____

_____

The Occasion: _____

Date: _____ Where: _____Time: _____

What was served: _____

Who Attended and What Did They Bring?   Food and/ or Gifts

On a scale of 1- 10, how successful was the gathering: _____

Games played: _____

Disagreements or arguments: _____

Other Notes: _____

_____

_____

_____

The Occasion: _____

Date: _____ Where: _____ Time: _____

What was served: _____

Who Attended and What Did They Bring?   Food and/ or Gifts

On a scale of 1- 10, how successful was the gathering: _____

Games played: _____

Disagreements or arguments: _____

Other Notes: _____

_____

_____

_____

The Occasion: _____

Date: _____ Where: _____Time: _____

What was served: _____

Who Attended and What Did They Bring?   Food and/ or Gifts

On a scale of 1- 10, how successful was the gathering: _____

Games played: _____

Disagreements or arguments: _____

Other Notes: _____

_____

_____

_____

The Occasion: _____

Date: _____ Where: _____Time: _____

What was served: _____

Who Attended and What Did They Bring?   Food and/ or Gifts

On a scale of 1- 10, how successful was the gathering: _____

Games played: _____

Disagreements or arguments: _____

Other Notes: _____

_____

_____

_____

The Occasion: _____

Date: _____ Where: _____Time: _____

What was served: _____

Who Attended and What Did They Bring?   Food and/ or Gifts

On a scale of 1- 10, how successful was the gathering: _____

Games played: _____

Disagreements or arguments: _____

Other Notes: _____

_____

_____

_____

The Occasion: _____

Date: _____ Where: _____Time: _____

What was served: _____

Who Attended and What Did They Bring?   Food and/ or Gifts

On a scale of 1- 10, how successful was the gathering: _____

Games played: _____

Disagreements or arguments: _____

Other Notes: _____

_____

_____

_____

Made in the USA
Lexington, KY
29 September 2018